EARLY POEMS

DOVER THRIFT EDITIONS

Ezra Pound

D0054509

DOVER PUBLICATIONS, INC.
MINEOLA, NEW YORK

DOVER THRIFT EDITIONS

GENERAL EDITOR: STANLEY APPELBAUM
EDITOR OF THIS VOLUME: THOMAS CROFTS

*The editors would like to thank
Prof. Richard Reid for his help in annotating this edition.*

Bibliographical Note

This Dover edition, first published in 1996, and reissued in 2015, is a new selection of Ezra pound's poems from the volumes *Personae* and *Exultations*, both originally published by Elkin Mathews, London, 1909; *Ripostes*, Small, Maynard and Company, Boston, 1913; *Cathay* (entire), Elkin Mathews, London, 1915; and *Hugh Selwyn Mauberly,* The Ovid Press, London, 1920. A new introductory Note, some explanatory footnotes (those in brackets) and an Alphabetical List of Titles and First Lines have been specially prepared for the present edition.

Library of Congress Catloging-in-Publication Data

Pound, Ezra, 1885–1972.
   [Poems. Selections]
   Early Poems / Ezra Pound.
      pages cm._(Dover thrift editions)
   Includes index.
   ISBN-13: 978-0-486-28745-4
   ISBN-10: 0-486-28745-9
   I. Title. II. Series

PS3531.082A6 1996
811'.52—dc20

95-16715
CIP

Manufactured in the United States by LSC Communications
28745905   2018
www.doverpublications.com

Note

EZRA LOOMIS POUND was born in Hailey, Idaho, in 1885, the only child of Homer Loomis Pound and Isabel Weston. In 1887 the Pounds moved east, Homer having accepted a job at the U.S. Mint in Philadelphia. Eventually, Pound went to the University of Pennsylvania where he studied Romance languages and was engaged in chess and fencing. Here, he also became friends with the young medical student and poet William Carlos Williams. Pound got his bachelor's degree after only two years of study and went on to post-graduate work, abandoning it however, in 1906, to begin a teaching career. He had become proficient in Greek, Latin, French, Italian, German, Spanish, Provençal and Anglo-Saxon.

After only a year teaching at Wabash Presbyterian College in Crawfordsville, Indiana, Pound was again on the move, this time to Europe. Between the years 1908 and 1910 he had published three books of poetry, *A Lume Spento*, *Personae* and *Exultations*; and a volume of criticism, *The Spirit of Romance*. In the years up to World War I, he became an influential contributor to two journals (*New Age* and *Poetry*), championed the careers of writers and artists (among them Robert Frost, D. H. Lawrence, James Joyce, T. S. Eliot and the sculptors Henri Gaudier-Brzeska and Jacob Epstein), made the acquaintance of Henry James (one of his idols) and advised William Butler Yeats on poetry. As well, he founded the school of Imagism, editing the anthology *Des Imagistes* in 1914. These years also saw the publication of more books of poetry and translations, as well as his marriage to Dorothy Shakespear of London. It is with the poetry of this period that the present selection is concerned, specifically the works *Personae* (1909), *Exultations* (1909), *Ripostes* (1913), *Cathay* (1915) and "Hugh Selwyn Mauberly" (1920).

In the volumes *Personae* and *Exultations* can be seen the poet's preoccupation with the Middle Ages. Both books contain poems set in the Crusades, dramatic monologues of medieval wanderer-poets and translations from Latin, Provençal, Italian and Spanish. Pound was cultivating a poetic practice similar to that of one of his favorite poets, Robert Browning, i.e. speaking through masks, "personae," allowing the poet to assume the personalities of various persons, historical or imaginative. Through this technique, the process of self-revelation occurs from the outside in, and is therefore an experience shared by the poet and the reader. Pound also shows himself an innovative love poet, at turns writing as a crusader to his sweetheart from abroad ("From Syria"); a spurned troubadour poet ("Na Audiart"); and even a delusional lycanthrope ("Pierre Vidal Old"). By combining the "man of action" with the passionate lover, Pound created some of the most *masculine* (while at the same time quite beautiful) love poems in the language.

In *Ripostes*, a collection of more varied settings, Pound's work is more deeply psychological. "The Tomb at Akr Çaar" is a haunting speech, set in a sealed Egyptian tomb; and the poem "Portrait d'une Femme," a complex psychological portrait, owes more than its title to Henry James (whom Pound early regarded a genius). This section also contains "The Seafarer," Pound's famous translation of the Anglo-Saxon poem, various songs and translations of Italy and France.

Working with the notes left by the (then) recently deceased orientalist Ernest Fenollosa (1853–1908), Pound, himself a scholar of Chinese poetry,[1] made a series of translations which he entitled *Cathay*. These pieces brought his lyric gift to bear in a totally new way. Here the poet's voice is further multiplied, and, in many cases, is softened somewhat, tempered by the quiet tones of Chinese poetry. If earlier in his career he had perfected the masculine love poem, *Cathay* gives us one of the most affecting *feminine* love poems ever: "The River Merchant's Wife: a Letter." *Cathay* added a new dimension to Pound's work, and, according to many, to English translation from Chinese in general. It is included here in its entirety. ("The Seafarer," however, originally included in *Cathay* to offer a comparison between contemporary poems from the Anglo-Saxon and the Chinese, has been reprinted here in its original context of the book *Ripostes* (1913).)

This selection ends with a piece from the last phase of the poet's early career. "Hugh Selwyn Mauberly" is Pound's "farewell to London." Disturbed by the condition of the arts, abuses of political power and the horrific slaughter of English and American youths in World War I, Pound wrote this embittered sequence of lyric pieces as a cry to the Anglo-American world in general. Though often sibilant and scornful, these poems do show the poet eloquent and passionate and in the grip of disturbing premonitions. This volume includes sections I–IX of this poem.

---

[1] Pound also edited and saw into print Fenollosa's book *The Chinese Written Character as a Medium for Poetry* (1936), and made his own translations of Confucius and others, including *Digest of the Analects* (1937) and *The Classical Anthology as Defined by Confucius* (1954).

Contents

From *Ripostes*, 1913

Cathay, 1915

From *Hugh Selwyn Mauberly*, 1920

Grace before Song

Lord God of heaven that with mercy dight
Th' alternate prayer-wheel of the night and light
Eternal hath to thee, and in whose sight
Our days as rain drops in the sea surge fall,

As bright white drops upon a leaden sea
Grant so my songs to this grey folk may be:

As drops that dream and gleam and falling catch the sun,
Evan'scent mirrors every opal one
Of such his splendour as their compass is,
So, bold My Songs, seek ye such death as this.

Cino

Italian Campagna 1309, the open road.

Bah! I have sung women in three cities,
But it is all the same;
And I will sing of the sun.

Lips, words, and you snare them,
Dreams, words, and they are as jewels,
Strange spells of old deity,
Ravens, nights, allurement:
And they are not;
Having become the souls of song.

Eyes, dreams, lips, and the night goes.
-Being upon the road once more,
They are not.
Forgetful in their towers of our tuneing
Once for Wind-runeing
They dream us-toward and
Sighing, say "Would Cino,
Passionate Cino, of the wrinkling eyes,
Gay Cino, of quick laughter,

1

Cino, of the dare, the jibe,
Frail Cino, strongest of his tribe
That tramp old ways beneath the sun-light,
Would Cino of the Luth were here!"

Once, twice, a year —
Vaguely thus word they:
            "Cino?" "Oh, eh, Cino Polnesi
            The singer is't you mean?"
            "Ah yes, passed once our way,
            A saucy fellow, but . . . .
            (Oh they are all one these vagabonds),
            Peste! 'tis his own songs?
            Or some other's that he sings?
            But *you*, My Lord, how with your city?"

But you "My Lord," God's pity!
And all I knew were out, My Lord, you
Were Lack-land Cino, e'en as I am
O Sinistro.

I have sung women in three cities.
But it is all one.
I will sing of the sun.
. . . . eh? . . . . they mostly had grey eyes,
But it is all one, I will sing of the sun.

        " 'Pollo Phoibee, old tin pan, you
        Glory to Zeus' aegis-day
        Shield o'steel-blue, th' heaven o'er us
        Hath for boss thy lustre gay!

        'Pollo Phoibee, to our way-fare
        Make thy laugh our wander-lied;
        Bid thy 'fulgence bear away care.
        Cloud and rain-tears pass they fleet!

        Seeking e'er the new-laid rast-way
        To the gardens of the sun . . . .

            .   .   .   .

            .   .   .   .

I have sung women in three cities
But it is all one.

I will sing of the white birds
In the blue waters of heaven,
The clouds that are spray to its sea.

Na Audiart[1]

Que be-m vols mal.

NOTE: Any one who has read anything of the troubadours knows well the tale of Bertran of Born and My Lady Maent of Montaignac, and knows also the song he made when she would none of him, the song wherein he, seeking to find or make her equal, begs of each preëminent lady of Langue d'Oc some trait or some fair semblance: thus of Cembelins her "esgart amoros" to wit, her love-lit glance, of Aelis her speech free-running, of the Viçomptess of Chales her throat and her two hands, at Roacoart of Anhes her hair golden as Iseult's; and even in this fashion of Lady Audiart "although she would that ill come unto him" he sought and praised the lineaments of the torse. And all this to make "Una dompna soiseubuda" a borrowed lady or as the Italians translated it "Una donna ideale."

Though thou well dost wish me ill
                            Audiart, Audiart,
Where thy bodice laces start
As ivy fingers clutching through
Its crevices,
                            Audiart, Audiart,
Stately, tall and lovely tender
Who shall render
                            Audiart, Audiart
Praises meet unto thy fashion?
Here a word kiss!
                            Pass I on
Unto Lady "Miels-de-Ben,"
Having praised thy girdle's scope,
How the stays ply back from it;
I breathe no hope
That thou shouldst . . . .
                            Nay no whit
Bespeak thyself for anything.
Just a word in thy praise, girl,
Just for the swirl
Thy satins make upon the stair,

---

[1] [*Na* is the Provençal equivalent of "Lady."]

'Cause never a flaw was there
Where thy torse and limbs are met:
Though thou hate me, read it set
In rose and gold,[1]
Or when the minstrel, tale half told,
Shall burst to lilting at the phrase
           "Audiart, Audiart" . . . .

Bertrans, master of his lays,
Bertrans of Aultaforte thy praise
Sets forth, and though thou hate me well,
Yea though thou wish me ill
                  Audiart, Audiart
Thy loveliness is here writ till,
                  Audiart,
Oh, till thou come again.[2]
And being bent and wrinkled, in a form
That hath no perfect limning, when the warm
Youth dew is cold
Upon thy hands, and thy old soul
Scorning a new, wry'd casement
Churlish at seemed misplacement
Finds the earth as bitter
As now seems it sweet,
Being so young and fair
As then only in dreams,
Being then young and wry'd,
Broken of ancient pride
Thou shalt then soften,
Knowing I know not how
Thou wert once she
                  Audiart, Audiart
For whose fairness one forgave
                  Audiart, Audiart
Que be-m vols mal.

---

[1] i. e. in illumed manuscript.
[2] Reincarnate.

Villonaud for This Yule

Towards the Noel that morte saison
(Christ make the shepherd's homage dear!)
Then when the grey wolves everychone
Drink of the winds their chill small-beer
And lap o' the snows food's gueredon
Then makyth my heart his yule-tide cheer
(Skoal! with the dregs if the clear be gone!)
Wineing the ghosts of yester-year.

Ask ye what ghosts I dream upon?
(What of the magians' scented gear?)
The ghosts of dead loves everyone
That make the stark winds reek with fear
Lest love return with the foison sun
And slay the memories that me cheer
(Such as I drink to mine fashion)
Wineing the ghosts of yester-year.

Where are the joys my heart had won?
(Saturn and Mars to Zeus drawn near!)[1]
Where are the lips mine lay upon,
Aye! where are the glances feat and clear
That bade my heart his valour don?
I skoal to the eyes as grey-blown mere
(Who knows whose was that paragon?)
Wineing the ghosts of yester-year.

Prince: ask me not what I have done
Nor what God hath that can me cheer
But ye ask first where the winds are gone
Wineing the ghosts of yester-year.

---

[1] Signum Nativitatis.

Ballad of the Gibbet: a Villonaud

Or the song of the sixth companion.

SCENE: *"En cest bourdel ou tenoms nostr estat."*
It being remembered that there were six of us with Master Villon, when
that expecting presently to be hanged he writ a ballad whereof ye know:
"Frères humains qui après nous vivez."[1]

Drink ye a skoal for the gallows tree!
Francois and Margot and thee and me,
Drink we the comrades merrily
That said us, "Till then" for the gallows tree!

Fat Pierre with the hook gauche-main,
Thomas Larron "Ear-the-less,"
Tybalde and that armouress
Who gave this poignard its premier stain
Pinning the Guise that had been fain
To make him a mate of the "Hault Noblesse"
And bade her be out with ill address
As a fool that mocketh his drue's disdeign.

Drink we a skoal for the gallows tree!
Francois and Margot and thee and me,
Drink we to Marienne Ydole,
That hell brenn not her o'er cruelly.

Drink we the lusty robbers twain,
Black is the pitch o' their wedding dress,[2]
Lips shrunk back for the wind's caress
As lips shrink back when we feel the strain
Of love that loveth in hell's disdeign
And sense the teeth through the lips that press
'Gainst our lips for the soul's distress
That striveth to ours across the pain.

---

[1] [*En cest . . .* : "In this bordello where we lodge." *Frères humains . . .* : "Human
brothers who live after us."]

[2] Certain gibbeted corpses used to be coated with tar as a preservative; thus one
scarecrow served as warning for considerable time. See Hugo "L'Homme qui Rit."

Drink we skoal to the gallows tree!
Francois and Margot and thee and me,
For Jehan and Raoul de Vallerie
Whose frames have the night and its winds in fee.

Maturin, Guillaume, Jacques d'Allmain,
Culdou lacking a coat to bless
One lean moiety of his nakedness
That plundered St. Hubert back o' the fane:
Aie! the lean bare tree is widowed again
For Michault le Borgne that would confess
In "faith and troth" to a traitoress
"Which of his brothers had he slain?"

But drink we skoal to the gallows tree!
Francois and Margot and thee and me:

These that we loved shall God love less
And smite alway at their faibleness?

Skoal!! to the Gallows! and then pray we:
God damn his hell out speedily
And bring their souls to his "Haulte Citee."

Scriptor Ignotus[1]

Ferrara 1715

TO K. R. H.

"When I see thee as some poor song-bird
Battering its wings, against this cage we call Today,
Then would I speak comfort unto thee,
From out the heights I dwell in, when
That great sense of power is upon me
And I see my greater soul-self bending
Sibylwise with that great forty-year epic
That you know of, yet unwrit
But as some child's toy 'tween my fingers,
And see the sculptors of new ages carve me thus,
And model with the music of my couplets in their hearts:

---

[1] [Unknown writer.]

Surely if in the end the epic
And the small kind deed are one;
If to God, the child's toy and the epic are the same,
E'en so, did one make a child's toy,
He might wright it well
And cunningly, that the child might
Keep it for his children's children
And all have joy thereof.

Dear, an this dream come true,
Then shall all men say of thee
"She 'twas that played him power at life's morn,
And at the twilight Evensong,
And God's peace dwelt in the mingled chords
She drew from out the shadows of the past,
And old world melodies that else
He had known only in his dreams
Of Iseult and of Beatrice.

Dear, an this dream come true,
I, who being poet only,
Can give thee poor words only,
Add this one poor other tribute,
This thing men call immortality.
A gift I give thee even as Ronsard gave it.
Seeing before time, one sweet face grown old,
And seeing the old eyes grow bright
From out the border of Her fire-lit wrinkles,
As she should make boast unto her maids
"Ronsard hath sung the beauty, *my* beauty,
          Of the days that I was fair."

So hath the boon been given, by the poets of old time
(Dante to Beatrice, — an I profane not —)
Yet with my lesser power shall I not strive
          To give it thee?

All ends of things are with Him
From whom are all things in their essence.
If my power be lesser
Shall my striving be less keen?
But rather more! if I would reach the goal,
          Take then the striving!
"And if," for so the Florentine hath writ

When having put all his heart
Into his "Youth's Dear Book"
He yet strove to do more honour
To that lady dwelling in his inmost soul
He would wax yet greater
To make her earthly glory more.
Though sight of hell and heaven were price thereof,
If so it be His will, with whom
Are all things and through whom
Are all things good,
Will I make for thee and for the beauty of thy music
A new thing
As hath not heretofore been writ.
     Take then my promise!

Comraderie

"*E tuttoque io fosse a la compagnia di molti, quanto alla vista.*"[1]

Sometimes I feel thy cheek against my face
Close-pressing, soft as is the South's first breath
That all the subtle earth-things summoneth
To spring in wood-land and in meadow space.

Yea sometimes in a bustling man-filled place
Me seemeth some-wise thy hair wandereth
Across mine eyes, as mist that halloweth
The air a while and giveth all things grace.

Or on still evenings when the rain falls close
There comes a tremor in the drops, and fast
My pulses run, knowing thy thought hath passed
That beareth thee as doth the wind a rose.

---

[1] ["And not withstanding that I was visibly in the company of many." Dante *La Vita Nuova*.]

Masks

These tales of old disguisings, are they not
Strange myths of souls that found themselves among
Unwonted folk that spake a hostile tongue,
Some soul from all the rest who'd not forgot
The star-span acres of a former lot
Where boundless mid the clouds his course he swung,
Or carnate with his elder brothers sung
Ere ballad-makers lisped of Camelot?

Old singers half-forgetful of their tunes,
Old painters colour-blind come back once more,
Old poets skilless in the wind-heart runes,
Old wizards lacking in their wonder-lore:

All they that with strange sadness in their eyes
Ponder in silence o'er earth's queynt devyse?

Xenia[1]

And
Unto thine eyes my heart
Sendeth old dreams of the spring-time,
Yea of wood-ways my rime
Found thee and flowers in and of all streams
That sang low burthen, and of roses,
That lost their dew-bowed petals for the dreams
We scattered o'er them passing by.

---

[1] [Foreign; *or* abroad]

Alba Belingalis[1]

Phoebus shineth ere his splendour flieth
Aurora drives faint light athwart the land
And the drowsy watcher crieth,

"ARISE."

Ref.

O'er cliff and ocean the white dawn appeareth
It passeth vigil and the shadows cleareth.

They be careless of the gates, delaying,
Whom the ambush glides to hinder,
Whom I warn and cry to, praying,

"ARISE."

Ref.

O'er cliff and ocean the white dawn appeareth
It passeth vigil and the shadows cleareth.

Forth from out Arcturus, North Wind bloweth
The stars of heaven sheathe their glory
And sun-driven forth-goeth

Settentrion.

Ref.

O'er sea mist, and mountain is the dawn display'd
It passeth watch and maketh night afraid.

From a tenth-century MS.

---

[1] MS. in Latin, with refrain,

"L alba par umet mar atras el poy
Pas abigil miraclar Tenebris."

It was and may still be the oldest fragment of Provençal known. [1909 note.]
[*Alba:* a medieval "morning" or "dawn" poem; *Belingalis:* bilingual, owing to MS.
in Latin and Provençal.]

From Syria

The song of Peire Bremon "Lo Tort" that he made for his Lady in
Provença: he being in Syria a crusader.

In April when I see all through
Mead and garden new flowers blow,
And streams with ice-bands broken flow,
Eke hear the birds their singing do;
When spring's grass-perfume floateth by
Then 'tis sweet song and birdlet's cry
Do make mine old joy come anew.

Such time was wont my thought of old
To wander in the ways of love.
Burnishing arms and clang thereof,
And honour-services manifold
Be now my need. Whoso combine
Such works, love is his bread and wine,
Wherefore should his fight the more be bold.

Song bear I, who tears should bring
Sith ire of love mak'th me annoy,
With song think I to make me joy.
Yet ne'er have I heard said this thing:
"He sings who sorrow's guise should wear."
Natheless I will not despair
That sometime I'll have cause to sing.

I should not to despair give way
That somewhile I'll my lady see.
I trust well He that lowered me
Hath power again to make me gay.
But if e'er I come to my Love's land
And turn again to Syrian strand,
God keep me there for a fool, alway!

God for a miracle well should
Hold my coming from her away,
And hold me in His grace alway
That I left her, for holy-rood.
An I lose her, no joy for me,

Pardi, hath the wide world in fee.
Nor could He mend it, if He would.

Well did she know sweet wiles to take
My heart, when thence I took my way.
'Thout sighing, pass I ne'er a day
For that sweet semblance she did make
To me, saying all in sorrow:
"Sweet friend, and what of me to-morrow?"
"Love mine, why wilt me so forsake?"

ENVOI

Beyond sea be thou sped, my song,
And, by God, to my Lady say
That in desirous, grief-filled way
My nights and my days are full long.
And command thou William the Long-Seer
To tell thee to my Lady dear,
That comfort be her thoughts among.

The only bit of Peire Bremon's work that has come down to us, and through its being printed with the songs of Giraut of Bornelh he is like to lose credit for even this. — E.P.

From the Saddle

D'Aubigné to Diane

Wearied by wind and wave death goes
With gin and snare right near alway
Unto my sight. Behind me bay
As hounds the tempests of my foes.
Ever on ward against such woes,
Pistols my pillow's service pay,
Yet Love makes me the poet play.
Thou know'st the rime demands repose,
So if my line disclose distress,
The soldier and my restlessness
And teen, Pardon, dear Lady mine,
For since mid war I bear love's pain
'Tis meet my verse, as I, show sign
Of powder, gun-match and sulphur stain.

And Thus in Nineveh

"Aye! I am a poet and upon my tomb
Shall maidens scatter rose leaves
And men myrtles, ere the night
Slays day with her dark sword.

"Lo! this thing is not mine
Nor thine to hinder,
For the custom is full old,
And here in Nineveh have I beheld
Many a singer pass and take his place
In those dim halls where no man troubleth
His sleep or song.
And many a one hath sung his songs
More craftily, more subtle-souled than I;
And many a one now doth surpass
My wave-worn beauty with his wind of flowers,
Yet am I poet, and upon my tomb
Shall all men scatter rose leaves
Ere the night slay light
With her blue sword.

"It is not, Raama, that my song rings highest
Or more sweet in tone than any, but that I
Am here a Poet, that doth drink of life
As lesser men drink wine."

Guido Invites You Thus[1]

"Lappo I leave behind and Dante too,
Lo, I would sail the seas with thee alone!
Talk me no love talk, no bought-cheap fiddl'ry,
Mine is the ship and thine the merchandise,
All the blind earth knows not th' emprise
Whereto thou calledst and whereto I call.

---

[1] The reference is to Dante's sonnet "Guido vorrei . . .

Lo, I have seen thee bound about with dreams,
Lo, I have known thy heart and its desire;
Life, all of it, my sea, and all men's streams
Are fused in it as flames of an altar fire!

Lo, thou hast voyaged not! The ship is mine."

Sestina: Altaforte

LOQUITUR: *En* Bertrans de Born.
    Dante Alighieri put this man in hell for that he was a stirrer-up of
      strife.
    Eccovi!
    Judge ye!
    Have I dug him up again?
The scene is at his castle, Altaforte. "Papiols" is his jongleur. "The Leop-
ard," the *device* of Richard (Cœur de Lion).[1]

I

Damn it all! all this our South stinks peace.
You whoreson dog, Papiols, come! Let's to music!
I have no life save when the swords clash.
But ah! when I see the standards gold, vair, purple, opposing
And the broad fields beneath them turn crimson,
Then howl I my heart nigh mad with rejoicing.

II

In hot summer have I great rejoicing
When the tempests kill the earth's foul peace,
And the light'nings from black heav'n flash crimson,
And the fierce thunders roar me their music
And the winds shriek through the clouds mad, opposing,
And through all the riven skies God's swords clash.

III

Hell grant soon we hear again the swords clash!
And the shrill neighs of destriers in battle rejoicing,
Spiked breast to spiked breast opposing!

---

[1] [*En* is the Provençal equivalent of "Sir." *Eccovi:* "There you are!" *Jongleur:*
jester, *also* minstrel *or* instrumental accompanist to a troubadour poet.]

Better one hour's stour than a year's peace
With fat boards, bawds, wine and frail music!
Bah! there's no wine like the blood's crimson!

IV

And I love to see the sun rise blood-crimson.
And I watch his spears through the dark clash
And it fills all my heart with rejoicing
And pries wide my mouth with fast music
When I see him so scorn and defy peace,
His lone might 'gainst all darkness opposing.

V

The man who fears war and squats opposing
My words for stour, hath no blood of crimson
But is fit only to rot in womanish peace
Far from where worth's won and the swords clash
For the death of such sluts I go rejoicing;
Yea, I fill all the air with my music.

VI

Papiols, Papiols, to the music!
There's no sound like to swords swords opposing,
No cry like the battle's rejoicing
When our elbows and swords drip the crimson
And our charges 'gainst "The Leopard's" rush clash.
May God damn for ever all who cry "Peace!"

VII

And let the music of the swords make them crimson!
Hell grant soon we hear again the swords clash!
Hell blot black for alway the thought "Peace"!

Piere Vidal Old

It is of Piere Vidal, the fool par excellence of all Provence, of whom the
tale tells how he ran mad, as a wolf, because of his love for Loba of
Penautier, and how men hunted him with dogs through the mountains of
Cabaret and brought him for dead to the dwelling of this Loba (she-wolf)

of Penautier, and how she and her Lord had him healed and made
welcome, and he stayed some time at that court. He speaks:

When I but think upon the great dead days
And turn my mind upon that splendid madness,
Lo! I do curse my strength
And blame the sun his gladness;
For that the one is dead
And the red sun mocks my sadness.

Behold me, Vidal, that was fool of fools!
Swift as the king wolf was I and as strong
When tall stags fled me through the alder brakes,
And every jongleur knew me in his song,
And the hounds fled and the deer fled
And none fled over long.

Even the grey pack knew me and knew fear.
God! how the swiftest hind's blood spurted hot
Over the sharpened teeth and purpling lips!
Hot was that hind's blood yet it scorched me not
As did first scorn, then lips of the Penautier!
Aye ye are fools, if ye think time can blot

From Piere Vidal's remembrance that blue night.
God! but the purple of the sky was deep!
Clear, deep, translucent, so the stars me seemed
Set deep in crystal; and because my sleep
— Rare visitor — came not, — the Saints I guerdon
For that restlessness — Piere set to keep

One more fool's vigil with the hollyhocks.
Swift came the Loba, as a branch that's caught,
Torn, green and silent in the swollen Rhone,
Green was her mantle, close, and wrought
Of some thin silk stuff that's scarce stuff at all,
But like a mist wherethrough her white form fought,

And conquered! Ah God! conquered!
Silent my mate came as the night was still.
Speech? Words? Faugh! Who talks of words and love?!
Hot is such love and silent,
Silent as fate is, and as strong until
It faints in taking and in giving all.

Stark, keen, triumphant, till it plays at death.
God! she was white then, splendid as some tomb
High wrought of marble, and the panting breath
Ceased utterly. Well, then I waited, drew,
Half-sheathed, then naked from its saffron sheath
Drew full this dagger that doth tremble here.

Just then she woke and mocked the less keen blade.
Ah God, the Loba! and my only mate!
Was there such flesh made ever and unmade!
God curse the years that turn such women grey!
Behold here Vidal, that was hunted, flayed,
·Shamed and yet bowed not and that won at last.

And yet I curse the sun for his red gladness,
I that have known strath, garth, brake, dale,
And every run-way of the wood through that great madness,
Behold me shrivelled as an old oak's trunk
And made men's mock'ry in my rotten sadness!

No man hath heard the glory of my days:
No man hath dared and won his dare as I:
One night, one body and one welding flame!
What do ye own, ye niggards! that can buy
Such glory of the earth? Or who will win
Such battle-guerdon with his "prowesse high"?

O Age gone lax! O stunted followers,
That mask at passions and desire desires,
Behold me shrivelled, and your mock of mocks;
And yet I mock you by the mighty fires
That burnt me to this ash.

. . . .
Ah! Cabaret! Ah Cabaret, thy hills again!

. . . .
Take your hands off me! . . . [*Sniffing the air.*
                    Ha! this scent is hot!

Ballad of the Goodly Fere[1]

Simon Zelotes speaketh it somewhile after the Crucifixion.

Ha' we lost the goodliest fere o' all
For the priests and the gallows tree?
Aye lover he was of brawny men,
O' ships and the open sea.

When they came wi' a host to take Our Man
His smile was good to see,
"First let these go!" quo' our Goodly Fere,
"Or I'll see ye damned," says he.

Aye he sent us out through the crossed high spears
And the scorn of his laugh rang free,
"Why took ye not me when I walked about
Alone in the town?" says he.

Oh we drank his "Hale" in the good red wine
When we last made company,
No capon priest was the Goodly Fere
But a man o' men was he.

I ha' seen him drive a hundred men
Wi' a bundle o' cords swung free,
That they took the high and holy house
For their pawn and treasury.

They'll no' get him a' in a book I think
Though they write it cunningly;
No mouse of the scrolls was the Goodly Fere
But aye loved the open sea.

If they think they ha' snared our Goodly Fere
They are fools to the last degree.
"I'll go to the feast," quo' our Goodly Fere,
"Though I go to the gallows tree."

"Ye ha' seen me heal the lame and blind,
And wake the dead," says he,

---

[1] Fere = Mate, Companion.

"Ye shall see one thing to master all:
'Tis how a brave man dies on the tree."

A son of God was the Goodly Fere
That bade us his brothers be.
I ha' seen him cow a thousand men.
I have seen him upon the tree.

He cried no cry when they drave the nails
And the blood gushed hot and free,
The hounds of the crimson sky gave tongue
But never a cry cried he.

I ha' seen him cow a thousand men
On the hills o' Galilee,
They whined as he walked out calm between,
Wi' his eyes like the grey o' the sea.

Like the sea that brooks no voyaging
With the winds unleashed and free,
Like the sea that he cowed at Genseret
Wi' twey words spoke' suddently.

A master of men was the Goodly Fere,
A mate of the wind and sea,
If they think they ha' slain our Goodly Fere
They are fools eternally.

I ha' seen him eat o' the honey-comb
Sin' they nailed him to the tree.

Hymn III

From the Latin of Marc Antony Flaminius, sixteenth century.

As a fragile and lovely flower unfolds its gleaming
        foliage on the breast of the fostering earth, if
        the dew and the rain draw it forth;
So doth my tender mind flourish, if it be fed with the
        sweet dew of the fostering spirit,
Lacking this, it beginneth straightway to languish,
        even as a floweret born upon dry earth, if the
        dew and the rain tend it not.

Portrait

From "La Mère Inconnue."[1]

Now would I weave her portrait out of all dim splendour.
Of Provence and far halls of memory,
Lo, there come echoes, faint diversity
Of blended bells at even's end, or
As the distant seas should send her
The tribute of their trembling, ceaselessly
Resonant. Out of all dreams that be,
Say, shall I bid the deepest dreams attend her?

Nay! For I have seen the purplest shadows stand
Alway with reverent chere that looked on her,
Silence himself is grown her worshipper
And ever doth attend her in that land
Wherein she reigneth, wherefore let there stir
Naught but the softest voices, praising her.

"Fair Helena" by Rackham

"What I love best in all the world?"

When the purple twilight is unbound,
        To watch her slow, tall grace
        and its wistful loveliness,
And to know her face
        is in the shadow there,
Just by two stars beneath that cloud —
The soft, dim cloud of her hair,
And to think my voice
        can reach to her

---

[1] ["The Unknown Mother."]

As but the rumour of some tree-bound stream,
Heard just beyond the forest's edge,
Until she all forgets I am,
And knows of me
Naught but my dream's felicity.

Francesca

You came in out of the night
And there were flowers in your hands,
Now you will come out of a confusion of people,
Out of a turmoil of speech about you.

I who have seen you amid the primal things
Was angry when they spoke your name
In ordinary places.
I would that the cool waves might flow over my mind,
And that the world should dry as a dead leaf,
Or as a dandelion seed-pod and be swept away,
So that I might find you again,
Alone.

Christophori Columbi Tumulus[1]

From the Latin of Hippolytus Capilupus, Early Cent. XVI.

Genoan, glory of Italy, Columbus thou sure light,
Alas the urn takes even thee so soon out-blown,
Its little space

Doth hold thee, whom Oceanus had not the might
Within his folds to hold, altho' his broad embrace
Doth hold all lands.

Bark-borne beyond his boundries unto Hind thou wast
Where scarce Fame's volant self the way had cast.

---

[1] [The Tomb of Christopher Columbus.]

Plotinus

As one that would draw through the node of things,
        Back sweeping to the vortex of the cone,
        Cloistered about with memories, alone
In chaos, while the waiting silence sings:

Obliviate of cycles' wanderings
        I was an atom on creation's throne
        And knew all nothing my unconquered own.
God! Should I be the hand upon the strings?!

But I was lonely as a lonely child.
I cried amid the void and heard no cry,
And then for utter loneliness, made I
New thoughts as crescent images of *me*.
And with them was my essence reconciled
While fear went forth from mine eternity.

On His Own Face in a Glass

O strange face there in the glass!
O ribald company, O saintly host!
O sorrow-swept my fool,
What answer? O ye myriad
That strive and play and pass,
Jest, challenge, counterlie?

I ?   I ?   I ?
                    And ye?

Histrion[1]

No man hath dared to write this thing as yet,
And yet I know, how that the souls of all men great
At times pass through us,
And we are melted into them, and are not

---

[1] [Actor.]

Save reflexions of their souls.
Thus am I Dante for a space and am
One François Villon, ballad-lord and thief
Or am such holy ones I may not write,
Lest blasphemy be writ against my name;
This for an instant and the flame is gone.

'Tis as in midmost us there glows a sphere
Translucent, molten gold, that is the "I"
And into this some form projects itself:
Christus, or John, or eke the Florentine;
And as the clear space is not if a form's
Imposed thereon,
So cease we from all being for the time,
And these, the Masters of the Soul, live on.

Defiance

Ye blood-red spears-men of the dawn's array
That drive my dusk-clad knights of dream away,
Hold! For I will not yield.

My moated soul shall dream in your despite
A refuge for the vanquished hosts of night
That *can* not yield.

A Song of the Virgin Mother

In the play "Los Pastores de Belen."[1] From the Spanish of Lope de Vega

As ye go through these palm-trees
O holy angels;
Sith sleepeth my child here
Still ye the branches.

O Bethlehem palm-trees
That move to the anger
Of winds in their fury,

---

[1] ["The Shepherds of Bethlehem."]

Tempestuous voices,
Make ye no clamour,
Run ye less swiftly,
Sith sleepeth the child here
Still ye your branches.

He the divine child
Is here a-wearied
Of weeping the earth-pain,
Here for his rest would he
Cease from his mourning,
Only a little while,
Sith sleepeth this child here
Stay ye the branches.

Cold be the fierce winds,
Treacherous round him.
Ye see that I have not
Wherewith to guard him,
O angels, divine ones
That pass us a-flying,
Sith sleepeth my child here
Stay ye the branches.

Planh for the Young English King[1]

   That is, Prince Henry Plantagenet, elder brother to Richard "Cœur de Lion."

   From the Provençal of Bertrans de Born "Si tuit li dol elh plor elh marrimen."

If all the grief and woe and bitterness,
All dolour, ill and every evil chance
That ever came upon this grieving world
Were set together they would seem but light
Against the death of the young English King.
Worth lieth riven and Youth dolorous,
The world o'ershadowed, soiled and overcast,
Void of all joy and full of ire and sadness.

---

[1] [*Planh*: lament.]

Grieving and sad and full of bitterness
Are left in teen the liegemen courteous,
The joglars supple and the troubadours.
O'er much hath ta'en Sir Death that deadly warrior
In taking from them the young English King,
Who made the freest hand seem covetous.
'Las! Never was nor will be in this world
The balance for this loss in ire and sadness!

O skilful Death and full of bitterness,
Well mayst thou boast that thou the best chevalier
That any folk e'er had, hast from us taken;
Sith nothing is that unto worth pertaineth
But had its life in the young English King,
And better were it, should God grant his pleasure
That he should live than many a living dastard
That doth but wound the good with ire and sadness.

From this faint world, how full of bitterness
Love takes his way and holds his joy deceitful,
Sith no thing is but turneth unto anguish
And each to-day 'vails less than yestere'en,
Let each man visage this young English King
That was most valiant mid all worthiest men!
Gone is his body fine and amorous,
Whence have we grief, discord and deepest sadness.

Him, whom it pleased for our great bitterness
To come to earth to draw us from misventure,
Who drank of death for our salvacioun,
Him do we pray as to a Lord most righteous
And humble eke, that the young English King
He please to pardon, as true pardon is,
And bid go in with honouréd companions
There where there is no grief, nor shall be sadness.

Alba Innominata[1]

From the Provençal.

In a garden where the whitethorn spreads her leaves
My lady hath her love lain close beside her,

---

[1] [Unnamed Dawn (or Dawn Song).]

Till the warder cries the dawn — Ah dawn that grieves!
Ah God! Ah God! That dawn should come so soon!
"Please God that night, dear night should never cease,
Nor that my love should parted be from me,
Nor watch cry 'Dawn' — Ah dawn that slayeth peace!
Ah God! Ah God! That dawn should come so soon!

"Fair friend and sweet, thy lips! Our lips again!
Lo, in the meadow there the birds give song!
Ours be the love and Jealousy's the pain!
Ah God! Ah God! That dawn should come so soon!

"Sweet friend and fair take we our joy again
Down in the garden, where the birds are loud,
Till the warder's reed astrain
Cry God! Ah God! That dawn should come so soon!

"Of that sweet wind that comes from Far-Away
Have I drunk deep of my Belovèd's breath,
Yea! of my Love's that is so dear and gay.
Ah God! Ah God! That dawn should come so soon!"

Envoi

Fair is the damsel and right courteous,
And many watch her beauty's gracious way.
Her heart toward love is no wise traitorous.
Ah God! Ah God! That dawn should come so soon!"

Silet[1]

When I behold how black, immortal ink
Drips from my deathless pen — ah, well-away!
Why should we stop at all for what I think?
There is enough in what I chance to say.

It is enough that we once came together;
What is the use of setting it to rime?
When it is autumn do we get spring weather,
Or gather may of harsh northwindish time?

---

[1] [It is silent.]

It is enough that we once came together;
What if the wind have turned against the rain?
It is enough that we once came together;
Time has seen this, and will not turn again;

And who are we, who know that last intent,
To plague to-morrow with a testament!

Apparuit[1]

Golden rose the house, in the portal I saw
thee, a marvel, carven in subtle stuff, a
portent. Life died down in the lamp and flickered,
        caught at the wonder.

Crimson, frosty with dew, the roses bend where
thou afar moving in the glamorous sun,
drinkst in life of earth, of the air, the tissue
        golden about thee.

Green the ways, the breath of the fields is thine there,
open lies the land, yet the steely going
darkly hast thou dared and the dreaded æther
        parted before thee.

Swift at courage thou in the shell of gold, cast-
ing a-loose the cloak of the body, camest
straight, then shone thine oriel and the stunned light
        faded about thee.

Half the graven shoulder, the throat aflash with
strands of light inwoven about it, loveli-
est of all things, frail alabaster, ah me!
        swift in departing.

---

[1] [It appeared.]

Clothed in goldish weft, delicately perfect,
gone as wind! The cloth of the magical hands!
Thou a slight thing, thou in access of cunning
       dar'dst to assume this?

The Tomb at Akr Çaar

"I am thy soul, Nikoptis. I have watched
These five millenia, and thy dead eyes
Moved not, nor ever answer my desire,
And thy light limbs, wherethrough I leapt aflame,
Burn not with me nor any saffron thing.

See, the light grass sprang up to pillow thee,
And kissed thee with a myriad grassy tongues;
But not thou me.

I have read out the gold upon the wall,
And wearied out my thought upon the signs.
And there is no new thing in all this place.

I have been kind. See, I have left the jars sealed,
Lest thou shouldst wake and whimper for thy wine.
And all thy robes I have kept smooth on thee.

O thou unmindful! How should I forget!
—Even the river many days ago,
The river, thou wast over young.
And three souls came upon Thee—

And I came.
And I flowed in upon thee, beat them off;
I have been intimate with thee, known thy ways.
Have I not touched thy palms and finger-tips,
Flowed in, and through thee and about thy heels?
How 'came I in'? Was I not thee and Thee?

And no sun comes to rest me in this place,
And I am torn against the jagged dark,
And no light beats upon me, and you say
No word, day after day.

Oh! I could get me out, despite the marks
And all their crafty work upon the door,
Out through the glass-green fields. . . .

. . . .

Yet it is quiet here:
I do not go."

Portrait d'une Femme

Your mind and you are our Sargasso Sea,
London has swept about you this score years
And bright ships left you this or that in fee:
Ideas, old gossip, oddments of all things,
Strange spars of knowledge and dimmed wares of price.
Great minds have sought you — lacking someone else.
You have been second always. Tragical?
No. You preferred it to the usual thing:
One dull man, dulling and uxorious,
One average mind — with one thought less, each year.
Oh, you are patient, I have seen you sit
Hours, where something might have floated up.
And now you pay one. Yes, you richly pay.
You are a person of some interest, one comes to you
And takes strange gain away:
Trophies fished up; some curious suggestion;
Fact that leads nowhere; and a tale or two,
Pregnant with mandrakes, or with something else
That might prove useful and yet never proves,
That never fits a corner or shows use,
Or finds its hour upon the loom of days:
The tarnished, gaudy, wonderful old work;
Idols and ambergris and rare inlays,
These are your riches, your great store; and yet
For all this sea-hoard of deciduous things,
Strange woods half sodden, and new brighter stuff:
In the slow float of differing light and deep,
No! there is nothing! In the whole and all,
Nothing that's quite your own.
                    Yet this is you.

The Seafarer

(From the early Anglo-Saxon text)

May I for my own self song's truth reckon,
Journey's jargon, how I in harsh days
Hardship endured oft.
Bitter breast-cares have I abided,
Known on my keel many a care's hold,
And dire sea-surge, and there I oft spent
Narrow nightwatch nigh the ship's head
While she tossed close to cliffs. Coldly afflicted,
My feet were by frost benumbed.
Chill its chains are; chafing sighs
Hew my heart round and hunger begot
Mere-weary mood. Lest man know not
That he on dry land loveliest liveth,
List how I, care-wretched, on ice-cold sea,
Weathered the winter, wretched outcast
Deprived of my kinsmen;
Hung with hard ice-flakes, where hail-scur flew,
There I heard naught save the harsh sea
And ice-cold wave, at whiles the swan cries,
Did for my games the gannet's clamour,
Sea-fowls' loudness was for me laughter,
The mews' singing all my mead-drink.
Storms, on the stone-cliffs beaten, fell on the stern
In icy feathers; full oft the eagle screamed
With spray on his pinion.
                                        Not any protector
May make merry man faring needy.
This he little believes, who aye in winsome life
Abides 'mid burghers some heavy business,
Wealthy and wine-flushed, how I weary oft
Must bide above brine.
Neareth nightshade, snoweth from north,
Frost froze the land, hail fell on earth then,
Corn of the coldest. Nathless there knocketh now
The heart's thought that I on high streams
The salt-wavy tumult traverse alone.

Moaneth alway my mind's lust
That I fare forth, that I afar hence
Seek out a foreign fastness.
For this there's no mood-lofty man over earth's midst,
Not though he be given his good, but will have in his youth greed;
Nor his deed to the daring, nor his king to the faithful
But shall have his sorrow for sea-fare
Whatever his lord will.
He hath not heart for harping, nor in ring-having
Nor winsomeness to wife, nor world's delight
Nor any whit else save the wave's slash,
Yet longing comes upon him to fare forth on the water.
Bosque taketh blossom, cometh beauty of berries,
Fields to fairness, land fares brisker,
All this admonisheth man eager of mood,
The heart turns to travel so that he then thinks
On flood-ways to be far departing.
Cuckoo calleth with gloomy crying,
He singeth summerward, bodeth sorrow,
The bitter heart's blood. Burgher knows not —
He the prosperous man — what some perform
Where wandering them widest draweth.
So that but now my heart burst from my breastlock,
My mood 'mid the mere-flood,
Over the whale's acre, would wander wide.
On earth's shelter cometh oft to me,
Eager and ready, the crying lone-flyer,
Whets for the whale-path the heart irresistibly,
O'er tracks of ocean; seeing that anyhow
My lord deems to me this dead life
On loan and on land, I believe not
That any earth-weal eternal standeth
Save there be somewhat calamitous
That, ere a man's tide go, turn it to twain.
Disease or oldness or sword-hate
Beats out the breath from doom-gripped body.
And for this, every earl whatever, for those speaking after —
Laud of the living, boasteth some last word,
That he will work ere he pass onward,
Frame on the fair earth 'gainst foes his malice,
Daring ado, . . .
So that all men shall honour him after
And his laud beyond them remain 'mid the English,

Aye, for ever, a lasting life's-blast,
Delight 'mid the doughty.
                              Days little durable,
And all arrogance of earthen riches,
There come now no kings nor Cæsars
Nor gold-giving lords like those gone.
Howe'er in mirth most magnified,
Whoe'er lived in life most lordliest,
Drear all this excellence, delights undurable!
Waneth the watch, but the world holdeth.
Tomb hideth trouble. The blade is layed low.
Earthly glory ageth and seareth.
No man at all going the earth's gait,
But age fares against him, his face paleth,
Grey-haired he groaneth, knows gone companions,
Lordly men are to earth o'ergiven,
Nor may he then the flesh-cover, whose life ceaseth,
Nor eat the sweet nor feel the sorry,
Nor stir hand nor think in mid heart,
And though he strew the grave with gold,
His born brothers, their buried bodies
Be an unlikely treasure hoard.

Echoes

I

Guido Orlando Singing

Befits me praise thine empery,
    Lady of Valour
Past all disproving;
Thou art the flower in me —
    Nay, by Love's pallor —
Of all good loving.

Worthy to reap men's praises
Is he who'd gaze upon
    Truth's mazes.
In like commend is he,
Who, loving fixedly,
Love so refineth,

Till thou alone art she
  In whom love's vested;
As branch hath fairest flower
  Where fruit's suggested.
This great joy comes to me,
  To me observing
How swiftly thou hast power
  To pay my serving.

II[1]

Thou keep'st thy rose-leaf
  Till the rose-time will be over,
    Think'st thou that Death will kiss thee?
Think'st thou that the Dark House
  Will find thee such a lover
As I? Will the new roses miss thee?

Prefer my cloak unto the cloak of dust
  'Neath which the last year lies,
For thou shouldst more mistrust
  Time than my eyes.

An Immortality

Sing we for love and idleness,
Naught else is worth the having,

Though I have been in many a land,
There is naught else in living.

And I would rather have my sweet,
Though rose-leaves die of grieving,

Than do high deeds in Hungary
To pass all men's believing.

---

[1] Asclepiades, Julianus Ægyptus.

Dieu! Qu'il la Fait

From Charles D'Orleans
For music

God! that mad'st her well regard her,
How she is so fair and bonny;
For the great charms that are upon her
Ready are all folk to reward her.

Who could part him from her borders
When spells are alway renewed on her?
God! that mad'st her well regard her,
How she is so fair and bonny.

From here to there to the sea's border,
Dame nor damsel there's not any
Hath of perfect charms so many.
Thoughts of her are of dream's order:
God! that mad'st her well regard her.

Δώρια[1]

Be in me as the eternal moods
            of the bleak wind, and not
As transient things are—
            gaiety of flowers.
Have me in the strong loneliness
            of sunless cliffs
And of grey waters.
            Let the gods speak softly of us
In days hereafter,
            The shadowy flowers of Orcus
Remember Thee.

---

[1] [*Dória*: in the Doric manner, or "things Doric."]

The Needle

Come, or the stellar tide will slip away.
Eastward avoid the hour of its decline,
Now! for the needle trembles in my soul!

Here have we had our vantage, the good hour.
Here we have had our day, your day and mine.
Come now, before this power
That bears us up, shall turn against the pole.

Mock not the flood of stars, the thing's to be.
O Love, come now, this land turns evil slowly.
The waves bore in, soon will they bear away.

The treasure is ours, make we fast land with it.
Move we and take the tide, with its next favour,
Abide
Under some neutral force
Until this course turneth aside.

The Picture[1]

The eyes of this dead lady speak to me,
For here was love, was not to be drowned out,
And here desire, not to be kissed away.

The eyes of this dead lady speak to me.

Of Jacopo del Sellaio

This man knew out the secret ways of love,
No man could paint such things who did not know.

And now she's gone, who was his Cyprian,
And you are here, who are "The Isles" to me.

And here's the thing that lasts the whole thing out:
The eyes of this dead lady speak to me.

---

[1] *"Venus Reclining,"* by Jacopo del Sellaio (1442–1493).

Song of the Bowmen of Shu

Here we are, picking the first fern-shoots
And saying: When shall we get back to our country?
Here we are because we have the Ken-nin for our foemen,
We have no comfort because of these Mongols.
We grub the soft fern-shoots,
When anyone says "Return," the others are full of sorrow.
Sorrowful minds, sorrow is strong, we are hungry and thirsty.
Our defence is not yet made sure, no one can let his friend return.
We grub the old fern-stalks.
We say: Will we be let to go back in October?
There is no ease in royal affairs, we have no comfort.
Our sorrow is bitter, but we would not return to our country.
What flower has come into blossom?
Whose chariot? The General's.
Horses, his horses even, are tired. They were strong.
We have no rest, three battles a month.
By heaven, his horses are tired.
The generals are on them, the soldiers are by them.
The horses are well trained, the generals have ivory arrows and
    quivers ornamented with fish-skin.
The enemy is swift, we must be careful.
When we set out, the willows were drooping with spring,
We come back in the snow,
We go slowly, we are hungry and thirsty,
Our mind is full of sorrow, who will know of our grief?

by Kutsugen.
4th Century B.C.

The Beautiful Toilet

Blue, blue is the grass about the river
And the willows have overfilled the close garden.
And within, the mistress, in the midmost of her youth,
White, white of face, hesitates, passing the door.
Slender, she puts forth a slender hand,

And she was a courtezan in the old days,
And she has married a sot,
Who now goes drunkenly out
And leaves her too much alone.

by Mei Sheng.
B.C. *140.*

The River Song

This boat is of shato-wood, and its gunwales are cut magnolia,
Musicians with jewelled flutes and with pipes of gold
Fill full the sides in rows, and our wine
Is rich for a thousand cups.
We carry singing girls, drift with the drifting water,
Yet Sennin needs
A yellow stork for a charger, and all our seamen
Would follow the white gulls or ride them.
Kutsu's prose song
Hangs with the sun and moon.

King So's terraced palace
        is now but a barren hill,
But I draw pen on this barge
Causing the five peaks to tremble,
And I have joy in these words
        like the joy of blue islands.
(If glory could last forever
Then the waters of Han would flow northward.)

And I have moped in the Emperor's garden, awaiting an order-
    to-write!
I looked at the dragon-pond, with its willow-coloured water
Just reflecting the sky's tinge,
And heard the five-score nightingales aimlessly singing.

The eastern wind brings the green colour into the island grasses at
    Yei-Shu,
The purple house and the crimson are full of Spring softness.
South of the pond the willow-tips are half-blue and bluer,
Their cords tangle in mist, against the brocade-like palace.
Vine-strings a hundred feet long hang down from carved railings,

And high over the willows, the fine birds sing to each other, and
    listen,
Crying—"Kwan, Kuan," for the early wind, and the feel of it.
The wind bundles itself into a bluish cloud and wanders off.
Over a thousand gates, over a thousand doors are the sounds of
    spring singing,
And the Emperor is at Ko.
Five clouds hang aloft, bright on the purple sky,
The imperial guards come forth from the golden house with their
    armour a-gleaming.
The Emperor in his jewelled car goes out to inspect his flowers,
He goes out to Hori, to look at the wing-flapping storks,
He returns by way of Sei rock, to hear the new nightingales,
For the gardens at Jo-run are full of new nightingales,
Their sound is mixed in this flute,
Their voice is in the twelve pipes here.

by Rihaku.
8th century A.D.

The River-Merchant's Wife: a Letter

While my hair was still cut straight across my forehead
I played about the front gate, pulling flowers.
You came by on bamboo stilts, playing horse,
You walked about my seat, playing with blue plums.
And we went on living in the village of Chokan:
Two small people, without dislike or suspicion.

At fourteen I married My Lord you.
I never laughed, being bashful.
Lowering my head, I looked at the wall.
Called to, a thousand times, I never looked back.

At fifteen I stopped scowling,
I desired my dust to be mingled with yours
Forever and forever and forever.
Why should I climb the look out?

At sixteen you departed,
You went into far Ku-to-Yen, by the river of swirling eddies,
And you have been gone five months.

The monkeys make sorrowful noise overhead.
You dragged your feet when you went out.
By the gate now, the moss is grown, the different mosses,
Too deep to clear them away!
The leaves fall early this autumn, in wind.
The paired butterflies are already yellow with August
Over the grass in the West garden;
They hurt me.
I grow older.
If you are coming down through the narrows of the river Kiang,
Please let me know beforehand,
And I will come out to meet you
                    As far as Cho-fu-Sa.

                                        by Rihaku.

The Jewel Stairs' Grievance

The jewelled steps are already quite white with dew,
It is so late that the dew soaks my gauze stockings,
And I let down the crystal curtain
And watch the moon through the clear autumn.

                                        by Rihaku.

NOTE. — Jewel stairs, therefore a palace. Grievance, therefore there is
something to complain of. Gauze stockings, therefore a court lady, not a
servant, who complains. Clear autumn, therefore he has no excuse on
account of weather. Also she has come early, for the dew has not merely
whitened the stairs, but has soaked her stockings. The poem is especially
prized because she utters no direct reproach.

Poem by the Bridge at Ten-Shin

March has come to the bridge head,
Peach boughs and apricot boughs hang over a thousand gates,
At morning there are flowers to cut the heart,
And evening drives them on the eastward-flowing waters.
Petals are on the gone waters and on the going,
                    And on the back-swirling eddies,

But to-day's men are not the men of the old days,
Though they hang in the same way over the bridge-rail.

The sea's colour moves at the dawn
And the princes still stand in rows, about the throne,
And the moon falls over the portals of Sei-go-yo,
And clings to the walls and the gate-top.
With head gear glittering against the cloud and sun,
The lords go forth from the court, and into far borders.
They ride upon dragon-like horses,
Upon horses with head-trappings of yellow metal,
And the streets make way for their passage.
                    Haughty their passing,
Haughty their steps as they go in to great banquets,
To high halls and curious food,
To the perfumed air and girls dancing,
To clear flutes and clear singing;
To the dance of the seventy couples;
To the mad chase through the gardens.
Night and day are given over to pleasure
And they think it will last a thousand autumns,
                    Unwearying autumns.
For them the yellow dogs howl portents in vain,
And what are they compared to the lady Riokushu,
                    That was cause of hate!
Who among them is a man like Han-rei
                    Who departed alone with his mistress,
With her hair unbound, and he his own skiffsman!

                                        by Rihaku.

Lament of the Frontier Guard

By the North Gate, the wind blows full of sand,
Lonely from the beginning of time until now!
Trees fall, the grass goes yellow with autumn.
I climb the towers and towers
                    to watch out the barbarous land:
Desolate castle, the sky, the wide desert.
There is no wall left to this village.
Bones white with a thousand frosts,

High heaps, covered with trees and grass;
Who brought this to pass?
Who has brought the flaming imperial anger?
Who has brought the army with drums and with kettle-drums?
Barbarous kings.
A gracious spring, turned to blood-ravenous autumn,
A turmoil of wars-men, spread over the middle kingdom,
Three hundred and sixty thousand,
And sorrow, sorrow like rain.
Sorrow to go, and sorrow, sorrow returning,
Desolate, desolate fields,
And no children of warfare upon them,
                    No longer the men for offence and defence.
Ah, how shall you know the dreary sorrow at the North Gate,
With Rihoku's name forgotten,
And we guardsmen fed to the tigers.

                                        by Rihaku.

Exile's Letter

To So-Kin of Rakuyo, ancient friend, Chancellor of Gen.
Now I remember that you built me a special tavern
By the south side of the bridge at Ten-Shin.
With yellow gold and white jewels, we paid for songs and laughter
And we were drunk for month on month, forgetting the kings and
        princes.
Intelligent men came drifting in from the sea and from the west
        border,
And with them, and with you especially
There was nothing at cross purpose,
And they made nothing of sea-crossing or of mountain crossing,
If only they could be of that fellowship,
And we all spoke out our hearts and minds, and without regret.

And then I was sent off to South Wei,
        smothered in laurel groves,
And you to the north of Raku-hoku,
Till we had nothing but thoughts and memories in common.

And then, when separation had come to its worst,
We met, and travelled into Sen-Go,

Through all the thirty-six folds of the turning and twisting waters,
Into a valley of the thousand bright flowers,
That was the first valley;
And into ten thousand valleys full of voices and pine-winds.
And with silver harness and reins of gold,
Out came the East of Kan foreman and his company.
And there came also the "True man" of Shi-yo to meet me,
Playing on a jewelled mouth-organ.
In the storied houses of San-ko they gave us more Sennin music,
Many instruments, like the sound of young phœnix broods.
The foreman of Kan-chu, drunk, danced because his long sleeves
        wouldn't keep still
With that music playing,
And I, wrapped in brocade, went to sleep with my head on his lap,
And my spirit so high it was all over the heavens,
And before the end of the day we were scattered like stars, or rain.
I had to be off to So, far away over the waters,
You back to your river-bridge.

And your father, who was brave as a leopard,
Was governor in Hei Shu, and put down the barbarian rabble.
And one May he had you send for me,
        despite the long distance.
And what with broken wheels and so on, I won't say it wasn't hard
        going,
Over roads twisted like sheep's guts.
And I was still going, late in the year, in the cutting wind from the
        North,
And thinking how little you cared for the cost, and you caring
        enough to pay it.
And what a reception:
Red jade cups, food well set on a blue jewelled table,
And I was drunk, and had no thought of returning.
And you would walk out with me to the western corner of the
        castle,
To the dynastic temple, with water about it clear as blue jade,
With boats floating, and the sound of mouth-organs and drums,
With ripples like dragon-scales, going grass green on the water,
Pleasure lasting, with courtezans, going and coming without hin-
        drance,
With the willow flakes falling like snow,
And the vermilioned girls getting drunk about sunset,

And the water a hundred feet deep reflecting green eyebrows
— Eyebrows painted green are a fine sight in young moonlight,
Gracefully painted —
And the girls singing back at each other,
Dancing in transparent brocade,
And the wind lifting the song, and interrupting it,
Tossing it up under the clouds.

> And all this comes to an end.
> And is not again to be met with.

I went up to the court for examination,
Tried Layu's luck, offered the Choyo song,
And got no promotion,

> and went back to the East Mountains
> white-headed.

And once again, later, we met at the South bridge-head.
And then the crowd broke up, you went north to San palace,
And if you ask how I regret that parting:

> It is like the flowers falling at Spring's end
> Confused, whirled in a tangle.

What is the use of talking, and there is no end of talking,
There is no end of things in the heart.

I call in the boy,
Have him sit on his knees here

> To seal this,

And send it a thousand miles, thinking.

by Rihaku.

From Rihaku

FOUR POEMS OF DEPARTURE

Light rain is on the light dust.
The willows of the inn-yard
Will be going greener and greener,
But you, Sir, had better take wine ere your departure,
For you will have no friends about you
When you come to the gates of Go.

Separation on the River Kiang

Ko-jin goes west from Ko-kaku-ro,
The smoke-flowers are blurred over the river.
His lone sail blots the far sky.
And now I see only the river,
      The long Kiang, reaching heaven.

Taking Leave of a Friend

Blue mountains to the north of the walls,
White river winding about them;
Here we must make separation
And go out through a thousand miles of dead grass.
Mind like a floating wide cloud.
Sunset like the parting of old acquaintances
Who bow over their clasped hands at a distance.
Our horses neigh to each other
            as we are departing.

Leave-Taking near Shoku

"Sanso, King of Shoku, built roads"

They say the roads of Sanso are steep,
Sheer as the mountains.
The walls rise in a man's face,
Clouds grow out of the hill
            at his horse's bridle.
Sweet trees are on the paved way of the Shin,
Their trunks burst through the paving,
And freshets are bursting their ice
            in the midst of Shoku, a proud city.

Men's fates are already set,
There is no need of asking diviners.

The City of Choan

The phœnix are at play on their terrace.
The phœnix are gone, the river flows on alone.
Flowers and grass
Cover over the dark path
        where lay the dynastic house of the Go.
The bright cloths and bright caps of Shin
Are now the base of old hills.

The Three Mountains fall through the far heaven,
The isle of White Heron
        splits the two streams apart.
Now the high clouds cover the sun
And I can not see Choan afar
And I am sad.

South-Folk in Cold Country

The Dai horse neighs against the bleak wind of Etsu,
The birds of Etsu have no love for En, in the north,
Emotion is born out of habit.
Yesterday we went out of the Wild-Goose gate,
To-day from the Dragon-Pen.[1]
Surprised. Desert turmoil. Sea sun.
Flying snow bewilders the barbarian heaven.
Lice swarm like ants over our accoutrements.
Mind and spirit drive on the feathery banners.
Hard fight gets no reward.
Loyalty is hard to explain.
Who will be sorry for General Rishogu,
            the swift moving,
Whose white head is lost for this province?

---

[1] *I.e.*, we have been warring from one end of the empire to the other, now east, now west, on each border.

Fragment[1]

You know very well where it was that I walked when you
    had left me.

Couplet

Drawing a sword, cut into water, water again flow:
Raise cup, quench sorrow, sorrow again sorry.

Hugh Selwyn Mauberley

(Life and Contacts)

E. P. ODE POUR L'ÉLECTION DE SON SÉPULCHRE[2]

"Vocat æstus in umbram"
Nemesianus, Ec. IV.[3]

I

For three years, out of key with his time,
He strove to resuscitate the dead art
Of poetry; to maintain "the sublime"
In the old sense. Wrong from the start—

No hardly, but seeing he had been born
In a half savage country, out of date;
Bent resolutely on wringing lilies from the acorn;
Capaneus; trout for factitious bait;

---

[1] [These two short pieces ("Fragment" and "Couplet") are taken from the end-notes of *Cathay* (1915).]

[2] ["Ode on the Selection of His Tomb"; cf. the poem of the same title by Pierre de Ronsard (1524–1585).]

[3] ["The heat invites us into the shade," from Eclogue IV of Nemesianus (active about 280 A.D.).]

῎Ιδμεν γάρ τοι πάνθ', ὅσ' ἐνὶ Τροίῃ[1]
Caught in the unstopped ear;
Giving the rocks small lee-way
The chopped seas held him, therefore, that year.

His true Penelope was Flaubert,
He fished by obstinate isles;
Observed the elegance of Circe's hair
Rather than the mottoes on sun-dials.

Unaffected by "the march of events,"
He passed from men's memory in *l'an trentiesme
De son eage;*[2] the case presents
No adjunct to the Muses' diadem.

II

The age demanded an image
Of its accelerated grimace,
Something for the modern stage,
Not, at any rate, an Attic grace;

Not, not certainly, the obscure reveries
Of the inward gaze;
Better mendacities
Than the classics in paraphrase!

The "age demanded" chiefly a mould in plaster,
Made with no loss of time,
A prose kinema, not, not assuredly, alabaster
Or the "sculpture" of rhyme.

III

The tea-rose tea-gown, etc.
Supplants the mousseline of Cos,
The pianola "replaces"
Sappho's barbitos.

Christ follows Dionysus,
Phallic and ambrosial
Made way for macerations;
Caliban casts out Ariel.

---

[1] ["For we know all of that [which did occur] in Troy"; from the sirens' song, Homer's *Odyssey* (Book 12).]

[2] ["The thirtieth year of his age"; an echo of a line in the first stanza of the *(Petit) Testament* of François Villon (1431–after 1462).]

All things are a flowing,
Sage Heracleitus says;
But a tawdry cheapness
Shall reign throughout our days.

Even the Christian beauty
Defects — after Samothrace;
We see τὸ καλόν[1]
Decreed in the market place.

Faun's flesh is not to us,
Nor the saint's vision.
We have the press for wafer;
Franchise for circumcision.

All men, in law, are equals.
Free of Pisistratus,
We choose a knave or an eunuch
To rule over us.

O bright Apollo,
τίν' ἄνδρα, τίν' ἥρωα, τινα θεόν,[2]
What god, man, or hero
Shall I place a tin wreath upon!

IV

These fought in any case,
and some believing, pro domo,[3] in any case . . .

Some quick to arm,
some for adventure,
some from fear of weakness,
some from fear of censure,
some for love of slaughter, in imagination,
learning later . . .

some in fear, learning love of slaughter;
Died some, pro patria, non "dulce" non "et decor" . . .[4]

---

[1] [The beautiful.]
[2] ["What man, what hero, what god" (Pindar).]
[3] ["For their home."]
[4] [The reference is to a famous passage in Horace: "*Dulce et decorum est pro patria mori* (Sweet and fitting it is to die for one's country)."]

walked eye-deep in hell
believing in old men's lies, then unbelieving
came home, home to a lie,
home to many deceits,
home to old lies and new infamy;

usury age-old and age-thick
and liars in public places.

Daring as never before, wastage as never before.
Young blood and high blood,
Fair cheeks, and fine bodies;

fortitude as never before

frankness as never before,
disillusions as never told in the old days,
hysterias, trench confessions,
laughter out of dead bellies.

V

There died a myriad,
And of the best, among them,
For an old bitch gone in the teeth,
For a botched civilization,

Charm, smiling at the good mouth,
Quick eyes gone under earth's lid,

For two gross of broken statues,
For a few thousand battered books.

Yeux Glauques[1]

Gladstone was still respected,
When John Ruskin produced
"King's Treasuries"; Swinburne
And Rossetti still abused.

---

[1] ["Sea-green eyes"; those of Elizabeth Siddal, who modeled for pre-Raphaelite painters and married Dante Gabriel Rossetti.]

Foetid Buchanan lifted up his voice
When that faun's head of hers
Became a pastime for
Painters and adulterers.

The Burne-Jones cartoons[1]
Have preserved her eyes;
Still, at the Tate, they teach
Cophetua to rhapsodize;

Thin like brook-water,
With a vacant gaze.
The English Rubaiyat was still-born
In those days.

The thin, clear gaze, the same
Still darts out faun-like from the half-ruin'd face,
Questing and passive. . . .
"Ah, poor Jenny's case"[2] . . .

Bewildered that a world
Shows no surprise
At her last maquero's
Adulteries.

"Siena mi fe'; Disfecemi Maremma"[3]

Among the pickled foetuses and bottled bones,
Engaged in perfecting the catalogue,
I found the last scion of the
Senatorial families of Strasbourg, Monsieur Verog.

For two hours he talked of Gallifet;
Of Dowson; of the Rhymers' Club;
Told me how Johnson (Lionel) died
By falling from a high stool in a pub . . .

[1] [i.e. drawings preparatory to a painting.]
[2] ["Jenny," prostitute-heroine from a poem by Rossetti.]
[3] ["Siena made me: Maremma unmade me" Dante's *Purgatory* V. 134.]

But showed no trace of alcohol
At the autopsy, privately performed —
Tissue preserved — the pure mind
Arose toward Newman as the whiskey warmed.

Dowson found harlots cheaper than hotels;
Headlam for uplift; Image impartially imbued
With raptures for Bacchus, Terpsichore and the Church
So spoke the author of "The Dorian Mood,"

M. Verog, out of step with the decade,
Detached from his contemporaries,
Neglected by the young,
Because of these reveries.

Brennbaum

The sky-like limpid eyes,
The circular infant's face,
The stiffness from spats to collar
Never relaxing into grace;

The heavy memories of Horeb, Sinai and the forty years,
Showed only when the daylight fell
Level across the face
Of Brennbaum "The Impeccable."

Mr. Nixon

In the cream gilded cabin of his steam yacht
Mr. Nixon advised me kindly, to advance with fewer
Dangers of delay. "Consider
          "Carefully the reviewer.

"I was as poor as you are;
"When I began I got, of course,
"Advance on royalties, fifty at first," said Mr. Nixon,
"Follow me, and take a column,
"Even if you have to work free.

"Butter reviewers. From fifty to three hundred
"I rose in eighteen months;
"The hardest nut I had to crack
"Was Dr. Dundas.

"I never mentioned a man but with the view
"Of selling my own works.
"The tip's a good one, as for literature
"It gives no man a sinecure.

"And no one knows, at sight, a masterpiece.
"And give up verse, my boy,
"There's nothing in it."

.   .   .   .

Likewise a friend of Bloughram's once advised me:[1]
Don't kick against the pricks,[2]
Accept opinion. The "Nineties" tried your game
And died, there's nothing in it.

---

[1] [cf. Robert Browning's "Bishop Bloughram's Apology."]
[2] ["I am Jesus whom thou persecutest: it is hard for thee to kick against the pricks." Acts 9:5.]

Alphabetical List of Titles
and First Lines